NORTH CAROLINA'S MOUNTAINS-TO-SEA TRAIL GUIDE

Gorges, Peaks, and Waterfalls
MST Segment 4

Black Mountain Campground to Beacon Heights

Compiled by Robert Trawick and Friends of the Mountains-to-Sea Trail

FRIENDS OF THE
**MOUNTAINS
-to-SEA TRAIL**
NORTH CAROLINA

www.MountainstoSeaTrail.org

Copyright © 2016 Friends of the Mountains-to-Sea Trail
ISBN: 978-0-89587-687-4

NORTH CAROLINA'S MOUNTAINS-TO-SEA TRAIL

Legend

Current Route

- ▬ *Trails*
- ▬ *Roads*
- ▬ *Paddle Route*
- ▬ *Optional Routes*

- ⬤ *Major Water Bodies*
- ⬤ *Municipal Boundaries*
- ⬤ *County Boundaries*
- ⬤ *Parks & Open Spaces*

Dear Friend of the MST:

The Mountains-to-Sea Trail (MST) provides an extraordinary way to explore North Carolina—one step at a time.

This booklet is one chapter of a trail guide for the entire MST written by Friends of the Mountains-to-Sea Trail (Friends). We have divided the trail into 18 segments, and each has a chapter like this one—with east and westbound directions; information about parking, camping, and other services; as well as background to help you learn more about the interesting areas of North Carolina through which the trail travels.

Chapters of the trail guide are available online at www.MountainstoSeaTrail. org/trail-guides, and printed book versions can be ordered on the Friends website, through the Friends' distributor—John F. Blair, Publisher (www.blairpub. com; 1-800-222-9796)—or from your local bookseller or online vendor.

Thanks to REI and Ecology Wildlife Foundation for generous

Current Trail Route

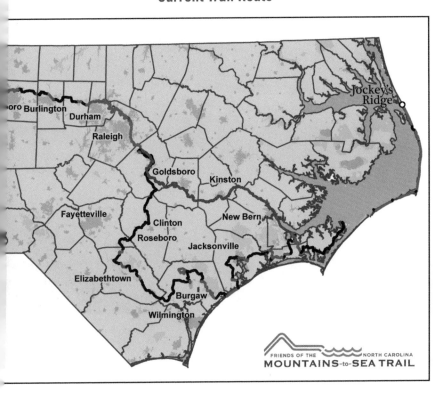

We hope you'll use this chapter and others to plan your next hikes on the MST. You may find a section of trail near your home to walk for the day. Or perhaps you will plan a weekend trip to hike the trail in a part of North Carolina you have never visited before. Or you may even undertake a challenging, inspiring trek of the entire 1,150-mile trail.

On the MST, you will experience North Carolina wilderness, wildlife, small towns, farms, and historic sites. You will enjoy rivers and islands, lakes and bays, urban greenways, ferries and forests, mountains and beaches. You will get a real feel for the sights, sounds, and people of North Carolina.

Please share your experiences on the trail and with this guide with Friends at info@MountainstoSeaTrail.org.

Happy Trails to You!
Kate Dixon, Executive Director

Linville Gorge on a good day
Photo by William Dolling

Gorges, Peaks, and Waterfalls—MST Segment 4

BLACK MOUNTAIN CAMPGROUND TO BEACON HEIGHTS
By Robert Trawick

Hikers on this 75-mile segment through the Pisgah National Forest follow forested ridgelines, climb peaks to dramatic views, forge rivers, and meander along creeks that lead to stunning waterfalls and crashing whitewater. The segment is very remote, with long departures from roads and little access to amenities.

Traveling eastbound, the trail leaves Black Mountain Campground on the South Toe River and climbs gradually to the Blue Ridge Parkway (BRP), at the Continental Divide to the Tennessee Valley. It travels through mostly mature forest in the Pisgah National Forest or along the BRP.

The trail then descends to the North Fork of the Catawba River and climbs Bald and Dobson Knobs, among the most challenging ascents on the entire MST. From these heights, hikers see some of the most spectacular views of the region, from Lake James to Little Switzerland.

The next part of the trail offers views of the impressive Linville Gorge, as it descends to the Linville River on the west side then climbs to the eastern lip of the gorge at Shortoff Mountain and follows its eastern edge. Because this popular part of the trail has had frequent forest fires, there are stretches with little water or shade from the Linville River until descending again at Table Rock.

The trail then dips into remote wild-trout waters located in areas nominated for wilderness status. It follows tributaries in the western Wilson Creek basin to the confluence of Harper and Raider Camp Creeks and then climbs along Harper Creek before hopping over a ridge to Lost Cove Creek and Gragg Prong. The trail follows these streams until it nears the BRP at Grandmother Mountain and Beacon Heights. Much of this part of the trail travels alongside crashing wild streams and rocky outcrops, which also offer picturesque cascades and waterfalls. This area was heavily timbered in the early 20th century and the trail often follows the old roads and railroad beds. One may look for traces of once vigorous human activity among the resurgent timber, in the sagging banks of these passages, and in the hints of washed-out and vanished bridges and settlements and wonder how nature has reclaimed these valleys and coves.

If you are interested in an overnight backpacking trip, this segment may be divided into 4 sections of roughly similar lengths. The first 19.6-mile section is between Black Mountain Campground and US 221 at the Forest Service Work Center at Woodlawn. The second 13.6-mile section is between US 221 at Woodlawn Work Center and Old NC 105. The third 19.5-mile section is between Old NC 105 and NC 181. The fourth 22.5-mile section is between NC 181 and Beacon Heights on the BRP.

HIGHLIGHTS INCLUDE

- Spectacular views of Linville Gorge, which drops 2,000 feet into the valleys below the ridges, as well as surrounding areas with views of Lake Tahoma, Lake James, and Pisgah National Forest

- Impressive promontories such as Dobson and Bald Knobs, the Pinnacle, the Chimneys, Shortoff Mountain, Table Rock, and Hawksbill

- Several waterfalls including Steels Creek, South Harper Creek, Harper Creek, Hunt Fish, and Gragg Prong Falls

South Harper Creek Falls on a cold January day, when the falls are partially frozen
Photo by Robert Trawick

Total Distance: 75.2 miles (73 miles are on trails or abandoned logging roads and less than 3 miles are on gravel roads)
Difficulty: Moderate to very difficult—the section hiking down and out of Linville Gorge from the Linville River is strenuous.

Trail Updates

When planning your trip using this guide, take a moment to see whether Friends of the Mountains-to-Sea Trail (Friends) has posted any updates about the trail route by visiting Friends' "Trail Updates" page at www. MountainstoSeaTrail.org/updates.

Camping on the Trail

With certain restrictions, camping is readily available on this trail segment, which falls almost entirely within the Pisgah National Forest. The only campground directly on the trail is listed below, followed by information about backpack camping along the trail.

Eastbound (EB) Mile 0.0; Westbound (WB) Mile 75.2
Black Mtn. Campground, 50 Black Mtn. Campground Rd., Burnsville, 28714, 828-675-5616. Open April-October, primitive sites, with water, restrooms, and showers. Camping is $22/night, first come, first serve. Cash or check only.

Except in the Linville Gorge Wilderness, Wilson Creek, and Lost Cove Creek areas, primitive camping is allowed anywhere in the Pisgah National Forest. A number of the most obvious backcountry sites are noted in the hiking directions below, but there has been no attempt to completely catalog all suitable sites.

In Linville Gorge Wilderness, Wilson Creek, and Lost Cove Creek areas, free camping permits are required on weekends and holidays from May 1-Oct. 31. Permits are not required Nov. 1-April 30 or for visitors who do not stay overnight. Reservations are taken on a first-come, first-serve basis, beginning the first working day of each previous month. For example, reservations for wilderness camping permits for June are accepted starting the first working day of May. Each visitor or group may get one weekend permit per month and may stay for up to three consecutive days and two nights.

Permits for campsites in Linville Gorge Wilderness, Wilson Creek, and Lost Cove Creek areas can be obtained from Grandfather Ranger District, 109 Lawing Drive, Nebo, 28761, 828-652-2144; grandfatherrd@fs.fed. us. Permits are issued by the district ranger office by mail or in person.

Regulations regarding camping near Linville Gorge Wilderness are at www.fs.usda.gov/generalinfo/nfsnc/recreation/camping-cabins/general info/?groupid=62891&recid=48974.

Camping is prohibited on all BRP property, which encompasses roughly EB Miles 5.3-8.1 and 74.8-75.2; WB Miles 0.0-0.4 and 67.1-69.9.

Before setting up a backcountry camp, please confirm that you are in a legal camping area.

Other Lodging and Campgrounds
Additional lodging within driving distance of the trail is available in Morganton and Marion and at other sites listed below. See the "Additional Information" section of this trail guide for tourism websites.

Near EB Mile 19.7; WB Mile 55.5 (4.0 miles south on US 221 to Marion; a few are listed here)
Sportsman Inn, 40 US 221, Marion, 28752, 828-659-7525.
Comfort Inn, 178 US 70W/221 Bypass/US 70 intersection, Marion, 28752, 828-652-4888.

Near EB Mile 19.7; WB Mile 55.5 or EB Mile 52.7; WB Mile 22.5
Blue Ridge View Farm. Aram and Linda Attarian make a loft apartment on their farm near Morganton available to MST hikers/backpackers. The loft has heat/AC, full bath, and an efficiency kitchen (no stove, has microwave, small refrigerator), and sleeps 4. They will provide shuttles. The cost is $80/night, and reservations can be made through Airbnb (look for Blue Ridge View Farm on the Airbnb website) or contact Aram Attarian directly at 919-815-8869. Be sure to mention that you are an MST hiker, and they will donate 10% of nightly fees to Friends.

Near EB Mile 52.7; WB Mile 22.5
10 miles from parking area at MP 21 on NC 181: Steele Creek Campground, 7081 NC 181, Morganton, 28655, 828-433-5660; www. steelecreekpark.com. $25; waterslide, swimming pool. Cash or check only. *Note:* the campground is spelled differently than the creek.

Near EB Mile 52.7; WB Mile 22.5

9 miles from parking area at MP 21 on NC 181: Daniel Boone Family Campground, 7360 NC 181, Morganton, 28655, 828-433-1200. No website and no cell service at campground but plenty of other amenities.

Near EB Mile 66.6; WB Mile 8.9

3 miles from Hunt Fish Falls parking area: US Forest Service Mortimer Campground www.fs.usda.gov/recarea/nfsnc/recreation/camping-cabins/recarea/?recid=49006&act; $10 nightly fee; flush toilets & showers; open April 1 to October 31.

Near EB Mile 75.2; WB Mile 0.0

3 miles south on US 221: Town of Linville.

8 miles east on the MST: campground at Grandfather Mtn. State Park, 9872 NC 105 S., Banner Elk, 28604, 828-963-9522. Primitive tent campsites have drinking water and fire rings. The park asks that you make a reservation by phone number above or online at www.ncparks.gov/Visit/parks/grmo/main.php

Food/Supplies/Services/Post Office

There are no amenities directly on the trail. The nearest towns are Linville, Marion, and Morganton.

EB Mile 19.7; WB Mile 55.5
(2.1 miles south on US 221)

KG's Quik Stop, 4613 US 221, Marion, 28753, 828-756-4975

Near EB Mile 52.7; WB Mile 22.5
(5.0 miles to Jonas Ridge)

Mountain Crossing Mercantile, 9041 NC 181, Jonas Ridge, 28641, 828-733-1488

Jonas Ridge post office, 9042 NC 18, 28641, 828-733-4711; weekdays 12:30 to 4:30; Saturday, 8:30 to 11:30

Camping Lodging Parking Food Restrooms Supplies Water Picnic

Near EB Mile 75.2; WB Mile 0.0 — Town of Linville is 3 miles south of BRP from Beacon Heights on US 221.

Linville post office, 4235 Mitchell Ave., 28646, 828-733-5745; weekdays 8:00 to noon & 1:00 to 4:00; Saturday, 8:00 to 11:30

Water/Restrooms

Water is generally abundant in this segment except between EB Mile 4.0 and EB Mile 16.7 (WB Mile 57.7 and WB Mile 71.2) where the trail follows a ridgeline. The hiking directions below do not attempt to catalog every potential source, keeping in mind that a decent-sized stream in wet weather may stop flowing completely in dry periods. Only larger, named creeks; those useful for wayfinding; and water sources in areas where they are more widely scattered are listed here. All surface water should be treated before drinking.

In addition to surface water on the trail, water and/or restrooms are available at the following sites.

EB Mile 0.0; WB Mile 75.2 — Black Mtn. Campground

EB Mile 19.7; WB Mile 55.5 — Woodlawn Work Center

EB Mile 44.3; WB Mile 30.9 — Table Rock Picnic Area

Hunting

Hunting is allowed throughout the Pisgah National Forest during hunting season and is prohibited on BRP property. Linville Gorge Wilderness Area is very popular as a hunting destination. See www.ncwildlife.org/hunting.aspx for information about seasons and licenses. During hunting season, hikers and any dogs accompanying them should wear blaze orange.

Signs/Blazing

Much of this segment travels through wilderness areas, so even MST blazing may be sparse. There is some signage along forest service roads in the vicinity of the Linville Gorge Wilderness Area. There are some blazed trails in the Harper Creek and Lost Cove Creek areas.

Camping Lodging Parking Food Restrooms Supplies Water Picnic

Special Considerations

The Linville River is approximately 60 yards wide at the crossing point. The water is usually at least knee deep, but it can be much higher and dangerous after rains and in cold weather. The hiking directions in this guide offer an alternate route to cross the river via a bridge if you reach the river when it is at dangerous levels.

There have been several major forest fires in this segment in recent years. As a result, there are sections where there are no large trees offering shade and some areas may appear rather desolate after the fires.

- All hikers should be able to identify and closely watch for two poisonous snakes—the copperhead and timber rattler.

- Fire can be a problem during dry periods. Please use fire rings and extinguish fires completely before leaving.

- Lock your car and carry valuables with you. Thieves can easily gain access to your car and its trunk.

- Carry a map and compass and let someone know where you plan to be and when you will return.

- Dogs are permitted on this segment, but should be leashed at all times.

ADDITIONAL INFORMATION

Friends office: 919-698-9024 or info@MountainstoSeaTrail.org

Pisgah National Forest:
www.fs.usda.gov/recarea/nfsnc/recarea/?recid=48114

Grandfather Ranger District, 109 Lawing Dr., Nebo, 28761, 828-652-2144

Appalachian Ranger District, 632 Manor Rd., Mars Hill, 28754, 828-698-9694

Linville Gorge: www.lgmaps.org

Yancey County: yanceychamber.com

McDowell County and Marion: www.mcdowellchamber.com

Burke County and Morganton: www.discoverburkecounty.com

Avery County and Linville: www.averycounty.com

Caldwell County and Lenoir: www.explorecaldwell.com

Trail Maps

Google map of entire MST: www.MountainstoSeaTrail.org/map

Linville Gorge and Mount Mitchell (National Geographic Map #779): www.natgeomaps.com/linville-gorge-mount-mitchell-pisgah-national-forest

South Toe River, Mount Mitchell and Big Ivy (US Forest Service): www.theforeststore.com/product/south-toe-river-mount-mitchell-big-ivy-trail-maps

Linville Gorge Wilderness (US Forest Service): www.theforeststore.com/product/linville-gorge-wildnerness

Wilson Creek/Harper Creek/Lost Cove Areas: Wilson Creek Visitor Center, 7805 Brown Mtn. Beach Rd., Collettsville, 28611, 828-759-0005; available at www.nationalforestmapstore.com/product-p/nc-16.htm

Other Valuable Links

Wilson Creek Visitor Center:
www.explorecaldwell.com/wilson-creek-visitor-center

Cradle of Forestry Interpretive Association: www.cfaia.org

Overmountain Victory Trail Association: www.nps.gov/ovvi

Ray's Weather: www.raysweather.com

Avery County: www.averyweather.com

McDowell County: www.mcdowellweather.com

PRIMARY PARKING LOCATIONS

Black Mtn. Campground on Forest Service Rd. (FS) 472 (South Toe River Rd.)
EB Mile 0.0; WB Mile 75.2
Ⓟ ⛺ 💧 🚻
N35.751262, W82.220684

Singecat Ridge Overlook (BRP Milepost [MP] 345.3)
EB Mile 6.2; WB Mile 69.0
Ⓟ
N35.756419, W82.176647

BRP Intersection with NC 80 at Buck Creek Gap (MP 344)
EB Mile 7.8; WB Mile 67.4
Ⓟ
N35.770427, W82.164191

Green Mtn. Rd. Opposite the Forest Service's Woodlawn Work Center
EB Mile 19.7; WB Mile 55.5
Ⓟ ⛱ 🚻
N35.767766, W82.042125

Bald Mtn. Trail Rd.
EB Mile 20.0; WB Mile 55.2
Ⓟ
N35.766256, W82.040740
Four-wheel drive to parking is advised. The gate for this road may be locked. Check with the ranger station at 828-652-2144 if you are hoping to park there.

FS 106 (Dobson Knob Rd.)
EB Mile 30.4; WB Mile 44.8
Ⓟ
N35.8200, W81.95942

Old NC 105/Kistler Memorial Hwy.
EB Mile 33.2; WB Mile 42.0
Ⓟ
N35.81415, W81.93758

Improved Parking Area Heading into Linville Gorge at the Pinnacle
EB Mile 34.0; WB Mile 41.2
Ⓟ
N35.82229, W81.93120

NC 126, Entrance to NC Wildlife Game Lands
EB Mile 37.1; WB Mile 38.1
Ⓟ
N35.80018, W81.88173

End of Wolf Pit Rd.
EB Mile 38.3; WB Mile 36.9
Ⓟ
N35.824155, W81.889419

Table Rock Parking Lot
EB Mile 44.3; WB Mile 30.9
Ⓟ ⛱ 🚻
N35.886467, W81.884597

Coordinates can be entered in your mapping software just like a street address.

 Camping Lodging Parking Food Restrooms Supplies Water  Picnic

PRIMARY PARKING LOCATIONS (Page 2)

FS 496 Just Before the Intersection with FS 210
EB Mile 46.3; WB Mile 28.9
Ⓟ
N35.896625, W81.869542

FS 496, 1.2 Miles from NC 181 at Ripshin Ridge
EB Mile 51.5; WB Mile 23.7
Ⓟ
N35.942106, W81.858103

NC 181 near FS 496 (MP 21)
EB Mile 52.7; WB Mile 22.5
Ⓟ
N35.952332, W81.846379

Brown Mtn. Beach Rd. (MP 7.0)
1.3 miles east of EB Mile 60.8;
WB Mile 14.4
Ⓟ
N35.977643, W81.766574

FS 464 (Pineola Rd.)
EB Mile 65.1; WB Mile 10.1
Ⓟ
N36.005759, W81.808519

FS 464 at Forest Service Trail (FST) 263 Parking Lot (Hunt Fish Falls)
EB Mile 65.6; WB Mile 9.6
Ⓟ
N36.0075, W81.801034

Roseborough Rd. Parking Area near FS 981
EB Mile 69.2; WB Mile 6.0
Ⓟ
N36.031273, W81.803718

Beacon Heights Parking Area (BRP MP 305.2)
EB Mile 75.2; WB Mile 0.0
Ⓟ
N36.08396, W81.83006

Coordinates can be entered in your mapping software just like a street address.

Camping Lodging Parking Food Restrooms Supplies ◆Water Picnic

Bridge on North Fork of Catawba River
Photo by Allen de Hart

Hiking Directions, Eastbound

0.0 From the parking area on FS 472 (South Toe River Rd.), take the trail past a kiosk, south up the slope, to begin Segment 4. The MST, Green Knob, and River Loop Trails are together at this point. *Note*: To reach the parking area by car from the BRP, take NC 80 (at MP 344) toward Burnsville. After the small community of Busick, turn left onto South Toe River Rd. This road will eventually turn to gravel and follow the river. At the gravel road intersection, make a slight turn on the first right. The parking area is on your left just before a bridge and the entrance to the Black Mtn. Campground on the right. See the "Camping on the Trail" section for this segment for information about camping at the Black Mtn. Campground. Ⓟ 🔺 💧 🚻

Camping Lodging Ⓟ Parking Food Restrooms Supplies 💧 Water Picnic

Segment 4 Eastbound

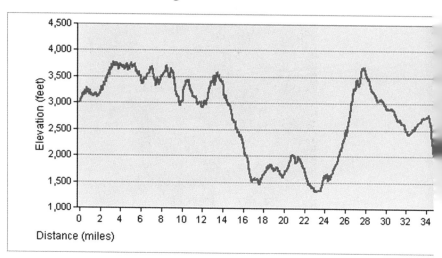

0.3 Green Knob Trail (FST 182) and River Loop Trail (FST 200) go right and south, MST continues east.

0.5 MST joins an old logging road.

1.0 The logging road splits and MST goes right.

1.2 Wildlife field is on the left.

1.3 MST goes right, leaving the logging road, which continues to FS 472.

1.4 Cross Lost Cove Creek. ●

1.5 Cross a rocky wet-weather streambed and then pass a wildlife field and old apple trees on the left.

1.6 Join an old logging road.

1.8 Arrive at a gate. The trail will join a logging road before crossing bridge over Neal's Creek. ●

2.0 Cross FS 2074 and pass through a gate onto an old logging road.

2.1 Trail climbs and offers a view of the Neal's Creek bowl.

2.2 MST leaves the old road, going right up the spine of the ridge, while an old road continues straight.

2.3 To the north-northwest, across the Toe River valley, there is a view of Maple Camp Bald and beyond it, 6,000-foot Cattail Peak. MST leaves the spine of the ridge going left, bending north with the contour.

▲Camping 🛏Lodging ℗ Parking 🍴Food 🚻Restrooms 📦Supplies ●Water ⛺Picnic

Elevation Profile

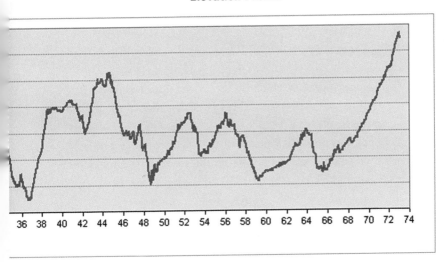

2.5 Trail follows an old road, which disappears when the trail narrows as the slope steepens. On the ridge, there is another view of the bowl, with the sound of the South Toe River in the background. You gradually climb this ridge through several wide switchbacks, which travel back and forth across its spine.

3.0 Cross over the ridge and leave the Neal's Creek basin.

3.1 To the northwest, across the valley, there is a view of the ridge with Balsam, Cattail Peak, Potato Hill, and Winterstar (L-R), all over 5,000 feet.

3.3 Trail goes through the gap between Big Laurel and Big Ridge, crossing into the Roaring Fork basin.

4.0 Cross a Roaring Fork tributary where there is camping downstream to the left. A 4,160-foot rocky peak looms to the south.

4.3 On a steep slope, the trail goes between boulders and over slick rocks.

4.4 Cross the remnants of an old logging road.

5.0 Trail goes parallel to a distinctive flat ridge to the south, which is the BRP.

5.3 After a gradual climb, reach a gap and then descend to BRP.

5.7 Cross the BRP. There is no parking access here.

6.1 MST follows a ridge south of BRP, heading east.

Camping Lodging Ⓟ Parking Food Restrooms Supplies 💧Water Picnic

6.2 Descend the ridge into the Singecat Overlook parking area (MP 345.3), where there is daytime access, and cross BRP again to the north and west. Ⓟ

6.6 Trail follows the ridge along BRP and then crosses again to the south and east.

7.6 Trail makes a gradual climb on top of the ridge beside BRP. When the trail turns north with the ridge, BRP passes through a tunnel underneath MST.

7.8 Trail empties onto BRP just west of a viaduct under which NC 80 passes at Buck Creek Gap. The trail heads east on BRP across the viaduct and exits, past the overpass, to the right onto an old road that climbs the ridge, parallel to BRP. Ⓟ

8.1 MST gains the top of the ridge in rhododendrons and swings away from BRP.

8.4 Reach a white gate just before a gap with views south. MST leaves an old road and goes right.

8.6 Trail makes an easy-to-moderate descent to a saddle where MST goes left, following the contours around the south and east side of the knob.

8.7 Reach Horse Gap where Armstrong Creek Trail (FST 223) goes north.

8.8 MST reaches the top of a knob with views back west to Buck Creek Gap before making a brief descent to a ridge across to the next knob.

9.0 Round the next knob and then make a moderate descent.

9.5 Reach a rounded knob and then descend to a saddle, continuing on the rounded ridge.

9.8 Make a moderate descent to the south side of a knob and then out onto a narrow ridge.

9.9 Reach a saddle with crossing trail, then continue, going up and skirting a knob on the right (south).

10.0 Trail is on a narrow ridgeback where it is level before making a moderate ascent of the next knob on left (north) side.

10.2 Trail takes switchbacks to climb the next knob, and then within 0.2 mile makes a moderate ascent to the top of another knob.

10.5 Trail levels out on top of the ridge, in rhododendrons going north. It then descends, switching back on the east side.

Ⓐ Camping ⛏ Lodging Ⓟ Parking 🍽 Food 🚻 Restrooms 🛒 Supplies 💧 Water ⛺ Picnic

Bald Knob looking toward Woodlawn
Photo by Bill Hodge

11.0 Trail is on top of the ridge and descends with the ridge to a gap in 0.2 mile, where there is a fire ring, before climbing the next knob on the left.

11.6 Trail is on top of a narrow ridge with views of Lake Tahoma before going left off the ridge.

12.5 Begin an ascent of Woods Mtn. along the ridge. Starting moderate, the climb will become strenuous with switchbacks and in 0.4 mile reaches the top where there is a fire ring and good views to the north.

13.1 Trail stays level on the ridge and then climbs some more. It will then descend around the peak and cross on a narrow ridge.

13.3 After a sharp ascent on the ridgeback, the trail goes left (north) around the knob, then turns hard right (south) on the east side.

13.4 A trail to the left leads to the site of the Woods Mtn. Lookout Tower. The only vestiges of the tower are the four concrete corner footings.

13.6 Make a moderate descent before the trail becomes wide with easy descent on rounded ridge.

13.9 Make a gradual descent on the left (east) side of the ridge. When the leaves are down there are good views to the east and southeast.

14.0 Trail wraps around the south end of the ridge and then descends moderately south and back east.

 Camping Lodging Parking Food Restrooms Supplies ◆ Water Picnic

Blazing Star over Linville Gorge
Photo by Adam Warwich

14.2 In a gap, where there is a fire ring, the trail goes right off the ridge. It begins a gradual-to-moderate descent on an old road.

14.4 MST is gradual to level, following the contour. Lake Tahoma is visible to the south.

14.9 Continue a gradual descent on an old road. Pass through scrubby burned-over pines.

15.3 Trail is still on an old road, passing through nice hardwoods. Another old road joins, coming up from left. MST continues a gradual descent on the contour.

15.5 The old road goes left while MST goes straight on the ridge. In 0.1 mile, a road comes in from the right and they both turn sharply left (east) and descend separately through an open hardwood forest.

16.0 In a gap, past interesting rock outcrops, MST goes left leaving the ridge. On the north side of the ridge, it enters rhododendron.

16.2 Return to the ridgeback and rejoin the road on a very wide corridor.

16.3 Leave the road and go left, following the ridge down in a moderate descent.

16.7 Make switchbacks, still descending, ending at a level and well-traveled road at South Fork of Tom's Creek. Go left. In a few hundred yards, cross a designated wild-trout stream, flowing left to right on a concrete ford. Continue on the road for 0.8 mile as it stays in the creek bottom, going upstream.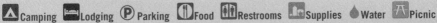

17.5 MST leaves the road, going right, and crosses a small creek, then the larger Tom's Creek. It briefly joins a wide trail going downstream before leaving the floodplain to go left up the hill, making a gradual climb up the western side of Grassy Knob.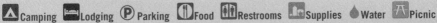

17.7 Reach an old road and go left.

18.4 Round the end of the ridge.

18.6 Join a well-traveled road coming from the right. Continue on this road for 1.0 mile.

19.6 MST is now close to US 221 at Woodlawn Park. Pass through stanchions into the park at the edge of a field. Trail goes right and switches back to descend to parking area at US 221 and the USFS Work Center at the community of Woodlawn.

19.7 Pass through the parking lot on Green Mtn. Rd. opposite the Woodlawn Work Center and go east to cross US 221. To the right (south) it is 2.0 miles to a convenience store on US 221; it is 4.0 miles to motels, restaurants, grocery store.

20.0 From US 221, the trail follows a rough, but traveled road, until it ends at a possible parking spot. Four-wheel drive is advised. The trail leaves the road on the right, going into rhododendrons. *Note:* The gate for this road may be locked. Check with the ranger station at 828-652-2144 if you are hoping to park there.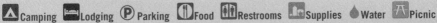

20.2 Other trails follow a dry streambed here, but MST takes a right across the stream and then makes a short climb to a wildlife field, which it skirts on the left (north and east).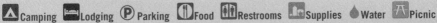

20.6 Past the field, the trail switches back and begins a climb, going into a pine forest.

20.9 Reach FS 149, where MST goes right on the road.

21.2 FS 149 reaches a T-intersection with FS 150. MST goes left on the road, up the hill.

21.4 Reach the rounded grassy summit where several roads intersect. Go left following one of the roads. Good camping.

 Camping Lodging Parking Food Restrooms Supplies Water Picnic

21.5 Arrive at the end of the road, which circles around the knob. MST goes left to descend to the North Fork of the Catawba River.

22.3 After a moderate descent, reach a good road coming down the hill from the right. MST goes left on the road, an easy descent along the contour.

22.6 Reach a creek and enter a floodplain, on the road.

22.9 Reach a gate at the edge of a field and a power-line corridor. In 100 yards, MST goes under the power lines and crosses a gravel maintenance road.

23.2 Trail bends left into the North Fork Catawba River floodplain, going upstream along an old road. 💧

23.5 Reach an entry to a nice 200-foot pedestrian bridge crossing the river. Leave the road to the right. The former crossing point for waders is 0.1 mile downstream.

23.6 Past the river, the trail crosses the railroad and begins a moderate climb.

23.8 Reach an old road, following the contour. Go left.

24.2 The road makes a gradual ascent, following the contours of the base of Bald Knob. As it makes turns around the mountain, there are occasional views of the valley, which the trail just crossed.

24.6 Leave the old road, going right into a hollow along an older road that follows a creek. 💧

24.7 There is a short path on right that leads to a piped spring. 💧

24.9 After an easy climb through open forest, the trail reaches the back of a ridge. It follows the ridge up, going left. In this area, there are several good camping spots. ⛺

25.2 The ridge becomes narrower and rock-strewn, but the climb has been easy to moderate.

25.4 Trail leaves the ridgetop to the left and crosses a rocky intermittent streambed.

25.6 Still climbing easy to moderate, reach a spot with a view to the west across the valley up to the Blue Ridge.

25.7 Pass a strange sinkhole on the left (uphill) side of the trail.

25.9 The climb has become moderate as the trail narrows on the steep slope.

Linville Gorge
Photo by Donnie Williams

26.2 Reach a rock outcrop with a spectacular view to the north and west. Looking uphill (east and north) you can see Bald Knob above and beyond (northeast) to Dobson Knob.

26.3 Very shortly, the trail reaches the top of a ridge with an overlook to the right with dramatic views to the south. The trail stays on top of the ridge and climbs moderately before beginning a series of rapid switchbacks.

26.5 Continuing switchbacks, the trail affords nice views to the north.

26.8 Trail reaches a very rugged fire road on the southwest-northeast spine and provides the first views of Lake James and the east. Go left on the spine, ascending.

26.9 Reaching the top of the knob, the trail continues to follow the sharp spine with only gradual changes in elevation.

27.1 Begin a series of dramatic rock outcrops with views to the west.

27.2 Begin a moderate descent of the northern end of Bald Knob, going into rhododendrons.

Camping Lodging Parking Food Restrooms Supplies Water Picnic

27.4 Trail sags to the east below the gap between the knobs, traveling in open forest.

27.5 Trail makes a short, strenuous climb back to the top of the ridge.

27.6 Trail reaches the top of the ridge.

27.7 Trail reaches the top of the knob, where there is a fire ring and a one-tent campsite. ▲

28.2 Trail makes a gradual descent on moss and then goes along a stream-bed. ⬤

28.3 Trail becomes an old, fairly level road.

28.4 A trail joins from the left.

28.5 The descent is steady, easy to moderate.

28.7 Still on the old road, the trail levels out into rhododendrons, then passes a wildlife field on the left. At an intersection of rutted roads, the trail goes straight, then left, following a road. There are campsites here. ▲

29.2 Pass a wildlife field on the left.

29.8 Trail continues on the road, which is badly rutted.

29.9 Campsite is on left at a bend in the road. ▲

30.4 Pass through a gate onto FS 106 (Dobson Knob Rd.) and reach a parking area. ℗

30.5 Reach two communication towers, then shortly a third.

31.5 Continue to follow FS 106. Pass a gated wildlife field on left with vehicle parking.

31.8 The Overmountain Victory Trail comes through a gate from the left and crosses FS 106, joining MST as it leaves FS 106 to the right onto an old road.

32.0 Trail leaves the old road to the left, where there is a nice campsite. ▲

32.2 After descending on a deeply rutted old road, cross a stream just below the juncture of two small streams. The trail makes a gradual climb to the ridge on the western edge of Linville Gorge. ⬤

32.9 Reach 2 small creeks. MST stays east of them. ⬤

33.2 Turn left off the old road into parking and access on Old NC 105 (SR 1238, also called Kistler Memorial Hwy.). MST leaves small parking area and goes left (north) on Old NC 105. ℗

34.0 After level-to-slight climb along the road, MST turns right at an improved parking area, heading toward the Linville Gorge. ℗

▲ Camping 🛏 Lodging ℗ Parking 🍴 Food 🚻 Restrooms 🏪 Supplies ⬤ Water ⛱ Picnic

34.3 Reach the Pinnacle, where a short trail goes right to an observation platform and rock outcrop with spectacular views to the east, south, and west. MST skirts the Pinnacle to the left (north) and begins a descent into the gorge on a ridge. Slope is burned over with little shade.

34.7 After a moderate-to-strenuous descent on the ridge, the trail's descent becomes gentler.

34.9 Before another sharp descent, the trail affords good views of Lake James and Shortoff Mtn.

35.1 Trail reaches a saddle and leaves the ridge going right, while another trail continues on the ridge up the other side of the saddle. The trail goes through open forest.

35.2 After a sharp descent from the saddle, reach a creek, which the trail will follow for 0.3 mile. 💧

35.4 Shortly, another creek flows in from the right. 💧

35.5 Trail goes left to cross the creek and to head up the slope toward the gorge.

35.7 Begin a climb up a knob separating the trail from the river.

35.9 After a moderate-to-strenuous climb with dramatic views of Shortoff Mtn., reach the top of the knob in thick young pines and begin the final descent to the river.

36.6 After a gentle-to-moderate descent, reach the river floodplain, where a trail joins from the right. Shortly, the trail reaches a road running along the river. MST goes right (south) on the road. Within a few hundred yards, MST turns left off the road, heading toward the river. *Note:* If the river is too high to cross, use the following route to reach a bridge to safely cross. Rather than take the MST, continue on the road 0.9 mile across private land to Parks Drive, which comes out on NC 126 at the Linville River bridge in another 0.3 mile. Going left (east) on NC 126, it is 0.7 mile to a NC Game Lands entrance on the left, where the blue-dot Linville River Connector Trail goes 2.5 miles to join the MST at EB Mile 41.1 on the slopes of Shortoff Mtn.

36.7 Reach the "Boy Scout" campsite beside the river where the trail goes left upstream. ⛺ 💧

36.8 Reach the west bank of the Linville River. The river is about 60 yards wide here and typically no more than knee high.

⛺ Camping   🛏 Lodging   Ⓟ Parking   🍴 Food   🚻 Restrooms   Supplies   💧 Water   ⛲ Picnic

36.8 Arrive on east bank of Linville River and begin hiking left, upstream through heavily used campsites and fire rings. ▲ 💧

36.9 Trail turns right and heads northeast away from the river. It begins a steady climb up the ridge that becomes Shortoff Mtn.

37.1 MST intersects with a blue-dot trail (Linville River Connector Trail), heading east (right) while MST goes straight up the ridge. On the connector trail, it is 2.5 miles to NC 126, a possible access point. At the NC 126 access location, there is a locked gate and limited parking at the entrance to NC Wildlife Game Lands. This trail forms an alternative route to avoid fording the Linville River by using NC 126 and Parks Drive. Ⓟ

37.4 You see the face of Shortoff Mtn. on the gorge side, and as the ridge narrows, you can also see Lake James.

38.2 Trail settles on the right (east) side of the ridge spine.

38.3 MST reaches a T-intersection with a trail from the right, which is accessible on Wolf Pit Rd. from NC 126. MST goes left toward the gorge and spectacular views. An alternate trail around the east side of Shortoff Mtn. goes straight, which reconnects with MST in 0.8 mile. Ⓟ

38.5 Trail swings west, giving a view of the gorge and peaks of the Black Mtns. to the west.

38.6 Trail levels out on the plateau, having climbed over 1,700 feet from the river. It now follows the lip of the gorge. It will not descend or ascend significantly for another 2.3 miles.

38.7 Trail follows a narrow passage, across a crevice and past a seep that is a possible, but not abundant, water source.

39.0 Traversing the rounded summit, the trail heads back east where there are many campsites. ▲

39.1 Lake James comes into view and the trail rejoins the alternate and goes left (north) along the ridge. MST goes through some rhododendron and some large living oaks. This area is level with camping spots. ▲

39.2 As the ridge narrows, the trail follows the rim where one can see down into the gorge with views of the Linville River and mountain ranges to the west.

39.3 Pass an unusual pond on top of the mountain; it is often dry.

▲Camping 🛏Lodging Ⓟ Parking 🍴Food 🚻Restrooms 🏬Supplies 💧Water 🏕Picnic

Wolf Pit and Shortoff Mtn.
Photo by Christine White

39.5 Trail passes through a desolate burned-over area with lots of downed wood and charred trunks where mountain laurel is the only live vegetation of any size.

40.8 There are views north of the Chimneys and Table Rock. The trail turns to right (east) and climbs to top of the ridge.

41.0 Begin the first descent since leaving the Linville River.

41.6 Trail follows a ridge, turning back west, with dramatic views to the north.

41.7 Reach the top of small knob.

41.9 Pass a fire ring on the ridge; the trees here have not been burned.

42.0 Sometimes easy to miss, MST turns sharp right to descend to Chimney Gap while Cambric Trail (FST 234), which is not maintained, follows the ridge west into the gorge.

42.1 Steady moderate descent.

42.3 Reach a saddle where there are campsites.

42.5 Pass through an area of severely burned pine, where all big trees are dead.

42.6 Reach an extensive campsite in the gap without a reliable water source.

42.7 Trail begins a steady climb to the Chimneys.

42.8 The climb is strenuous, but quickly reaches a small saddle.

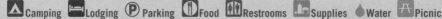

43.1 Dramatic overlook with a view of the east side of the ridge up to Table Rock.

43.6 Trail turns right to the north, following the west side of the ridge with views of the gorge and river, looking along the gorge side of the Chimneys and to Table Rock ahead.

43.9 Trail follows the west side of the ridge into the Chimneys, passing around and among remarkable shapes and stacks of rock.

44.0 Trail goes on top of the ridge past the Chimneys.

44.1 Descend to an extensive and heavily used camping area. 🔺

44.3 Reach the south side of the Table Rock parking lot where there are trash receptacles, vault toilets, and picnic tables, but no water. On FS 210, it is 13 miles to NC 181. MST continues from the north side of the parking lot and combines with a trail to climb Table Rock. Ⓟ 🚻

44.7 MST and Table Rock Trail turn right to follow a ridge up, while Little Table Rock Trail (FST 236) goes left and follows the ridge down. At this junction, there is a spring directly ahead and down the mountainside. In less than 100 yards, MST will go left to continue around the mountain while the Table Rock Trail goes right to continue its ascent. 💧

45.4 MST descends gradually and at this point begins a moderate descent through open mature forest with a view of Hawksbill straight ahead.

45.6 Reach a series of wooden steps and enter a campsite where an old road goes left to Spence Ridge Trail (FST 233) and FS 210. MST goes right and joins a small stream. 🔺 💧

45.8 Reach FS 210, where MST goes right along the road about 200 feet before turning left to continue its descent along a tributary of Buck Creek. 💧

46.2 Reach FS 496 and go right.

46.3 Trail leaves FS 496 just before the intersection with FS 210. MST goes left. Ⓟ

46.7 Trail climbs a small knob and you can hear Buck Creek to the left.

46.9 Trail rounds a ridge and levels out.

47.0 Reenter rhododendron and descend sharply before leveling out into a cove.

47.3 Trail tees into another trail, which is often overgrown. Go left.

47.5 Trail enters an opening in the forest with a fire pit on the left, a possible camping spot.

47.6 Trail is squeezed beside rock faces on the right and a steep rhododendron slope to the left.

47.9 Small streams and springs cross the trail during the wet season. ●

48.3 After hugging the north side of a ridge, the trail rises and stays on top for 0.1 mile, then cuts left, descending the slope, then switches back.

48.4 After following the ridge, the trail cuts back left (west) so that the slope is from left to right, and you can hear the creek.

48.5 Another trail joins from left and crosses MST. It will re-cross in a few 100 yards. This old road will descend on top of the ridge while MST stays on south side. Follow blazes.

48.7 After a moderate descent, reach a floodplain where there is good camping to the right. Follow the trail left through open forest where there is more camping. ▲

48.8 Cross Buck Creek, flowing left to right just before it joins Steels Creek. There are many fishing trails to the right going downstream. MST does not cross Steels Creek, but follows it upstream on the west side, climbing the slope where possible to stay out of the flood zone.

48.9 Trail comes even with Steels Creek. Look for blazes that show where the trail climbs the slope to the left; they may be difficult to find. ●

49.1 Trail stays above and away from creek, but here they are forced together through a narrows and then climb rapidly.

49.4 Trail arrives at a floodplain with good camping spots. The trail then leaves the creek and camping area, switching back to climb the slope. Steels Creek Falls is 100 yards upstream from the camping area and worth the side trip, which requires climbing over a few boulders. ▲ ●

49.7 Trail goes through open forest of maples and poplars with lush fern ground cover.

50.2 Trail follows an old road and passes a wildlife field with apple trees to the left.

50.3 Trail reaches Steels Creek tributary, Gingercake Creek, where there is good camping. Very shortly, you cross Steels Creek. ▲ ●

50.4 Trail merges with another road coming in from the right.

50.6 Re-cross Steels Creek, where there are good campsites. ▲ ●

▲ Camping 🛏 Lodging Ⓟ Parking 🍴 Food 🚻 Restrooms 🛒 Supplies ● Water ⛺ Picnic

51.0 Trail leaves the creek and goes into a pine, magnolia, and oak forest where it begins to climb a ridge dividing Steels Creek and Gingercake Creek.

51.3 Trail continues a moderate climb and reaches the end of the ridge.

51.4 You reach the end of a road spur from FS 496. Head through a notch to the right. Once through the notch, stay left. An old trail goes right.

51.5 Pass through locked gate onto FS 496, where parking is possible. To the right on FS 496 it is 1.2 miles to NC 181 at Ripshin Ridge. Ⓟ

51.9 Pass a fire ring and campsite where the old MST comes in from right. You can take this side trip to Steels Creek Falls. △

52.7 FS 496 terminates at NC 181 and MST crosses the highway, over the guardrails and into the forest. There is a parking area on the east side of NC 181, just north of MP 21. It is 5.0 miles north on NC 181 to general store and post office; 10.0 miles to full-service private campgrounds. After leaving NC 181, the trail bears right through rhododendron and emerges into a wildlife field. △ Ⓟ 🏬

52.8 Trail begins a descent on a 2-3-foot-deep, washed-out gully.

52.9 Trail, which has been following just north of a ridge, crosses at a saddle and turns right and begins a descent beside a small creek on the right. 💧

53.2 Trail crosses a small creek, flowing left to right into the main creek and levels out, entering open forest with good camping spots. △

53.3 Trail descends with the creek along rock outcrops, which make nice picnic spots. The creek falls away quickly to the right.

53.6 Cross a small spring as the trail follows the south side of a slope.

53.8 Trail bottoms out and rejoins a much larger creek. There are many side trails to the creek. Upper Creek comes in from the left and the trail follows it upstream a short distance to a crossing point. Good camping area. This area is known as Greentown where there was once a post office during the logging days. △ 💧

53.9 Trail turns right and crosses the creek. Rock-hopping is possible. The trail then turns right on the other side and follows it downstream, entering a rhododendron tunnel before moving away from the creek.

54.1 Trail levels out into open forest of poplars and maples.

54.4 Trail crosses one of many small creeks, some with culverts, some with timbers.

Bridge over North Fork of Catawba River
Photo by Mark Moser

54.5 Trail follows the south and east slope with occasional views across the valley to Chestnut Mtn. The slope is steep to the right while the trail moves in and out of deciduous forest and rhododendron thickets.

56.3 Merge onto FS 198 coming from the right. Pass through a gate. This area, with good campsites, is known as Wilderness Camp. Although you will see improved parking here, vehicle travel on FS 198 is generally blocked at FS 982 to prevent travel on an extremely rough road.

56.4 Merge into an old road and follow it left. You will see an improved parking area on the left and come to another gate. This road will widen and continue for about 0.5 mile. Blazes may be hard to find here due to overgrowth, but the trail follows a north-south corridor along the old roadbed.

57.1 The road ends and MST crosses another trail with blue vertical-rectangular blazes, which join the white dots of MST. The blue-blaze trail goes right to Chestnut Mtn. The MST goes straight, and

Camping Lodging Parking Food Restrooms Supplies Water Picnic

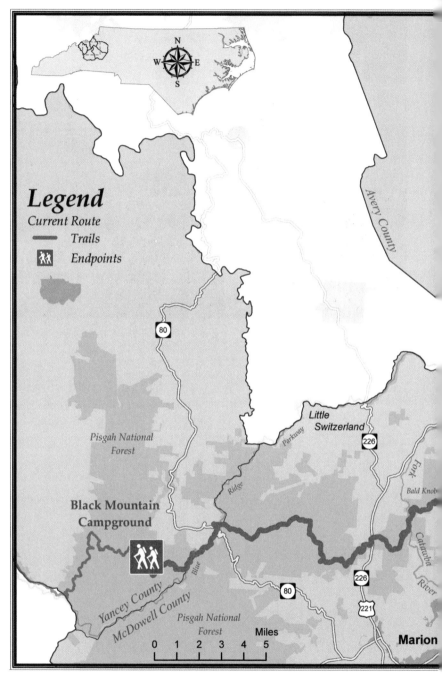

Map and elevation profile produced for Friends of the Mountains-to-Sea Trail by Curtis Belyea, 2016.

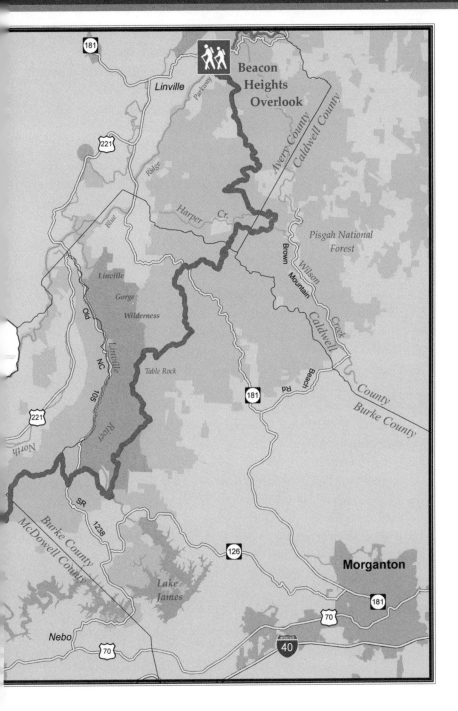

181

Linville

Parkway

Beacon
Heights
Overlook

221

Avery County

Caldwell County

Ridge

Blue

Harper Cr.

Pisgah National
Forest

Brown

Wilson

Mountain

Linville

Gorge

Wilderness

Caldwell

Creek

Table Rock

181

Beach Rd

County

Burke County

Old

Linville

NC

105

River

221

North

SR

1238

Burke County

McDowell County

126

Morganton

181

Lake
James

Nebo

70

70

40

INTERSTATE

will dip into the Harper Creek basin before coming into the Raider Camp Creek basin on the other side of Chestnut Mtn.

58.1 MST turns right, following the contour while the other trail continues straight and upward through a notch. MST soon enters rhododendron and mountain laurel and wraps left around the slope on a narrow ledge while giving views to the northeast.

58.2 After descending, MST crosses the ridge and is rejoined by a trail from the left; MST continues straight and descends several hundred yards further to join a trail on the contour, which it follows, going right. It then follows a broad rounded ridge gently downhill through mature forest.

58.3 Trail, which has been in a deep narrow gully, now levels out onto a flat trail and reaches a T-intersection where MST goes right onto an old railroad bed.

58.4 Good camping spots. Magnificent large oaks.

58.5 Trail leaves the top of the ridge and descends gradually, going north. Shortly it reaches a T-intersection with FST 277 (Raider Camp Creek Trail). MST joins this trail going right. Left, it is 0.2 mile to a cliff overlooking South Harper Creek with a dramatic view into a box canyon and the 250-foot South Harper Falls. On the north side of the creek, approximately 200 feet below, is the Harper Creek Trail (FST 260), which is reachable from FS 58 going to Kawana (a former community designated on Forest Service maps).

58.6 Trail emerges from a mature forest into a burned-over recovering forest of scrubby growth. It turns east around a bend, affording panoramic views of mountains to the north from west-to-east, including Grandmother and Grandfather Mtns.

58.9 Trail ascends to a saddle, where it crosses a trail following the ridge. MST continues straight and begins to descend into the Raider Camp basin in an open forest of mature hardwoods, predominantly poplar.

59.8 The descent slows as the trail nears Raider Camp Creek. The trail follows the creek until it meets Harper Creek, dropping rapidly in places.

Camping Lodging ⓟ Parking Food 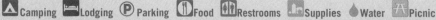Restrooms Supplies ◆Water Picnic

Harper Creek Falls
Photo by Robert Trawick

60.3 Trail emerges onto a floodplain where there are plentiful campsites. It then passes through an open rhododendron valley with lush moss and dog hobble before reaching Harper Creek. ⛺ 💧

60.8 Reach Harper Creek, which usually cannot be rock-hopped without getting wet. MST crosses the creek, going east into an extensive and heavily used camping area. Enter the clearing on the western edge of the campsite, go left and ascend on an old railroad bed. There is an access to this campground from a parking area at Mile 7 on Brown Mtn. Beach Rd. (SR 1328); the parking area is 1.3 miles east on red-blazed FST 260. Ⓟ ⛺ 💧

61.0 Trail hugs a slope and rises over 30 yards above the creek as the gorge narrows. As it climbs the slope, a trail goes straight, following an old railroad bed. Within 100 yards, this trail ends at an overlook of Harper Creek Falls, a series of 15-foot falls.

61.3 The gorge widens and the trail levels out, coming closer to the creek. Good camping sites. ⛺ 💧

61.4 Trail crosses a small stream, flowing right to left, and passes by a level camping spot as it follows a sunny overgrown margin of the creek. ⛺

⛺Camping 🛏Lodging Ⓟ Parking 🍴Food 🚻Restrooms 🛒Supplies 💧Water ⛱Picnic

61.5 Trail crosses the creek to the west side, where there is a campsite and fire ring; rock-hopping may be possible. Trail goes right upstream. You may see signs of a railroad including rails and a railbed.

61.8 Cross the creek again from west to east side.

62.1 Trail is in an open mature hardwood forest with level camping spots 30-40 feet from the creek. ⛺ 💧

62.6 Trail crosses the creek again at a shallow spot from east to west and goes right upstream and then soon crosses back to the east side and goes left upstream.

62.7 Reach a wide spot under mature hardwoods with fire rings and camping spots. ⛺ 💧

62.8 Trail crosses creek again from east to west.

63.0 Reach a level open area on west side of creek with camping area big enough for 1-2 tents, shortly before crossing back from west to east. ⛺ 💧

63.1 Cross the creek east-to-west and reach a wide extensive camping area under hollies. ⛺ 💧

63.5 Trail is 50 feet above the creek, where it flows as a white sheet of water over the rocks. For the next 0.1 mile the trail stays on a steep slope beside the creek as it crashes through the cascades and among large rock outcrops below. Picturesque picnic spot.

63.9 Cross the creek again from west to east.

64.0 Trail enters open mature forest with possible campsites. ⛺ 💧

64.1 MST turns right and away from creek; blue blazes are visible going straight, the continuation of North Harper Creek Trail (FST 266A). MST soon begins to climb a ridge to FS 464. Over the next mile, the trail climbs, winding in and out of steep coves among big oaks, maples, and pines.

64.6 Trail crosses a ridge and heads left on the north and east side.

65.1 Emerge into a clearing and go left to reach the road, then right on the road (FS 464 or Pineola Rd.). Ⓟ

65.6 Reach a pullout and improved parking with a sign for "Hunt Fish Falls" indicating the trail is also FST 263. Trail leaves road to left (north). For 0.7 mile the trail will descend through mostly rhododendron to Lost Cove Creek. Ⓟ

66.0 Trail begins to follow a small creek. 💧

⛺ Camping 🛏 Lodging Ⓟ Parking 🍴 Food 🚻 Restrooms 🏪 Supplies 💧 Water ⛱ Picnic

Hunt Fish Falls
Photo by Kenneth Johnson

66.3 Trail reaches Lost Cove Creek near the top of Hunt Fish Falls, where there are two small falls of 6-8 feet. The trail goes right, following the creek downstream. There are possible campsites. Within 100 yards, the trail crosses the base of Hunt Fish Falls, where the creek that the trail followed down the slope from Pineola Rd. flows over a series of falls 50 feet high. ▲ ●

66.7 Trail opens out into broad plain with lots of camping and fire rings. The trail continues, hugging the slope away from the creek. ▲ ●

66.9 Cross the creek and go right.

67.0 Timber Ridge Trail (FST 261) comes down the slope from Timber Ridge from the left and joins MST as it continues downstream. In a few 100 yards, leave Lost Cove Creek before it meets Gragg Prong and go left (north), climbing a bank, going up the west side of Gragg Prong.

▲ Camping 🛏 Lodging Ⓟ Parking 🍴 Food 🚻 Restrooms 🎒 Supplies ● Water 🛉 Picnic

67.2 Cross Gragg Prong west to east and go upstream on a narrow trail on the slope.

67.3 Pass a fire ring beside the creek.

67.8 Trail, which has been 20-40 yards above the creek on the slope, now descends to an area of good swimming, wading, sunning at 35-foot Gragg Prong Falls, a series of rocks and falls.

67.9 A nice rock juts out into the creek.

68.0 Campsite down at the creek at the foot of another falls series with rock outcrops and pools.

68.1 Cross Gragg Prong from east to west.

68.2 Cross again, rock-hopping, west to east.

68.3 Pass by an overlook a few yards from the trail. Here you can see Gragg Prong flow rapidly through a narrow rock sluice 20 yards below.

68.6 Pass a fire ring and campsite beside the creek.

68.7 Another nice side trail to rocks and rapids where there is a 3-foot cataract and several pools.

68.8 Cross Gragg Prong from east to west.

68.9 Trail clings to the slope above the creek in places, where across the creek there are heavily used car camping areas on FS 981/SR 1511.

69.2 Reach the parking area near Roseborough. Follow the drive out of parking lot to road (FS 981), then right across bridge over Gragg Prong and left up washed-out FS 192 on the east side of Gragg Prong. Ⓟ

70.0 Road is relatively straight and wide and climbs steadily. It reaches a knoll where 25 yards to the left there is a campsite and fire ring. The road then descends slightly or stays level for a short distance.

70.2 Road comes back within earshot of Gragg Prong, still to the west. There is a campsite and water source, where a tributary of Gragg Prong crosses the road.

70.4 Pass private posted land with a gate on the left.

70.6 Trail steadily climbs on the road.

70.8 You can hear Gragg Prong far below.

71.5 Trail is within 50 yards of Gragg Prong.

71.6 A road on the left goes 200 yards to a campsite beside the creek.

Gragg Prong Falls
Photo by John Mitchell

71.8 Road comes within 10 yards beside and 15 yards above Gragg Prong. The road will leave Gragg Prong as it climbs to Old House Gap.

72.1 The road forks, with MST going to the right and another road continuing left to a gate. Stay right.

72.3 A spur goes left to a campsite.

72.4 Reach a crossroads at Old House Gap. MST goes left on FST 4053, which passes through a white gate, climbing on the ridge and crossing to the north side on an old road.

72.5 On the north side of the ridge, there are views across the valley to BRP and Grandfather Mtn. beyond.

72.8 On the old overgrown road, trail is level at first, then with a moderate steady climb in a washed-out center of the road.

73.0 MST leaves the old road and goes right around the north and east side of ridge while road continues straight on the south side. As it curves around to the north side, the trail enters rhododendrons.

73.5 Trail descends into the cove and crosses one of the many small tributaries of Andrews Creek.

73.7 Another small stream crossing.

73.8 Reach another stream, which the trail follows in an eroded gully before crossing it and beginning to climb out on north side of the cove.

74.1 Up and over a finger of the ridge into the next cove.

74.3 Cross a small stream.

74.4 Cross the stream again, climbing out of the cove.

74.6 The climb becomes strenuous in stretches.

74.8 Fabulous overlook to the south and east.

75.0 Join rocky road from Grandmother Mtn. Rd., coming in from the left.

75.1 Beacon Heights Trail goes right to Beacon Heights. Be sure to take this short detour because the views from the rock outcroppings encompass Grandfather Mtn. and a large portion of Pisgah National Forest.

75.2 Tanawha Trail begins to run conjunctively with MST; the eastern end of Segment 4 is 130 yards to the left at Beacon Heights parking area (BRP MP 305.2). *Note:* The parking area is 4 miles east of Linville. From Linville, take US 221 toward the BRP. You pass Grandfather Mtn. entrance after 2 miles; 2 more miles at intersection with BRP, turn south and go 0.5 mile to parking area on left. Ⓟ

Falls along Gragg Prong
Photo by Robert Trawick

Hiking Directions, Westbound

0.0 Segment 4 starts at the Beacon Heights parking area (BRP MP 305.2), where the MST begins running eastward conjunctively with the Tanawha Trail. From the parking area, cross gravel road and follow signs to Beacon Heights. When the trail intersects with Tanawha Trail, turn right. *Note:* The parking area is 4 miles east of Linville. Take US 221 toward the BRP. You pass Grandfather Mtn.

Camping Lodging Parking Food Restrooms Supplies Water Picnic entrance after 2 miles; 2 more miles at intersection with BRP, turn south and go 0.5 mile to parking area on left. Ⓟ

0.1   Beacon Heights Trail goes left to spectacular views from bald rock outcrops to the southeast.

0.2   MST goes left, descending, as the rocky road continues to Grandmother Mtn. Rd. (SR 1513).

0.4   Fabulous overlook to the south and east as the descent continues.

0.6   Drop is rapid in stretches.

0.8   Cross a very small stream. 💧

0.9   Encounter the stream again.

1.1   Travel over a ridge into the next cove.

1.4   Cross another stream and follow it in an eroded gully.

1.5   Come to another small stream crossing. These are tributaries of Andrews Creek.

1.7   Leave a small creek and begin a moderate climb out of the cove. 💧

2.2   Coming out of rhododendrons on the north side of a ridge, and rounding its east end, MST joins an old impassable road (FS 4053) coming from the right on the south side of the ridge.

2.4   Make a moderate descent on the old overgrown road, which is washed out in the center.

2.7   Views back to the left (north) across the valley to BRP and Grandfather Mtn. and beyond.

2.8   Mount the ridge and descend on its crest until passing through a white gate to reach a crossroads at Old House Gap. MST goes right on FS 192 and descends for 3.0 miles. This road is passable and sometimes traveled, but very rugged.

2.9   A spur road goes right to a campsite.

3.1   Another road goes back sharply to the right, continuing to a gate. Continue straight.

3.4   The road comes within 10 yards beside and 15 yards above Gragg Prong. The trail will stay within a few hundred yards of Gragg Prong for the next 5 miles.

3.6   A road goes left 200 yards to a campsite beside the creek. 🔺 💧

3.7   Near Gragg Prong again.

4.4   You can hear Gragg Prong far below.

4.6   The trail steadily descends on the road.

🔺Camping 🛏Lodging Ⓟ Parking 🍴Food 🚻Restrooms 🏪Supplies 💧Water ⛺Picnic

Hunt Fish Falls
Photo by Donnie Williams

4.8 Private posted land with a gate is on the right.

5.0 The road comes back within earshot of Gragg Prong, which is still to the west. There is a campsite and water source where a tributary of Gragg Prong crosses the road. ⬩

5.2 Brief climb to a knoll; on right is a campsite and fire ring. The road becomes relatively straight and wide. ⬩

6.0 Reach relatively well-travelled FS 981 near Roseborough. There is a heavily used parking and camping area along creek straight ahead. Go right and cross the bridge over Gragg Prong. MST then goes left and reaches a parking area. MST then hugs the west and south side of Gragg Prong. ⬩ Ⓟ ⬩

6.3 The trail clings to the slope across from the camping area.

6.4 Cross Gragg Prong from west to east.

6.5 There is a nice side trail to rocks and rapids where there is a 3-foot cataract and several pools.

6.6 A fire ring and campsite are located beside the creek. ⬩ ⬩

6.9   Pass by an overlook a few yards from the trail. Twenty yards below, Gragg Prong flows rapidly through a narrow rock sluice.

7.0   Cross Gragg Prong, rock-hopping, east to west.

7.1   Cross west to east, rock-hopping.

7.2   Campsite down at the creek at the foot of another falls series with rock outcrops and pools. ▲ ◖

7.3   A nice rock juts out into the creek.

7.4   The trail reaches an area of good swimming, wading, sunning at 35-foot Gragg Prong Falls, a series of rocks and falls, then ascends to stay 20-40 yards above the creek.

7.9   There is a fire ring beside the creek.

8.0   From a narrow trail on the slope, descend to the creek and cross it east to west.

8.2   Descend a bank to the confluence with Lost Cove Creek and go right, upstream along the north side of Lost Cove, where within 100 yards Timber Ridge Trail (FST 261) departs going right uphill. MST continues upstream along Lost Cove.

8.3   Cross to the south side of Lost Cove Creek, rock-hopping.

8.5   Enter a level plain beside the creek with lots of campsites and fire rings. ▲ ◖

8.9   A small tributary of Lost Cove Creek falls 50 feet from the slope to the left. In 100 yards, reach Hunt Fish Falls, two small falls of 6-8 feet. There are possible campsites here. Near the top of the falls, MST goes left up the slope. It climbs moderately 0.7 mile to Pineola Rd. ▲ ◖

9.2   Leave the small tributary. ◖

9.6   Reach moderately well-traveled Pineola Rd. (FS 464) at an improved parking area. MST goes right on FS 464 for 0.5 mile. ℗

10.1 Leave FS 464 to the left in a clearing. For the next mile, MST winds in and out of steep coves among big oaks, maples, and pines. ℗

10.6 Cross a ridge.

11.1 Reach Harper Creek in a flat floodplain. Blue blazes of FST 266A go right upstream, and MST goes left downstream on the north side of the creek. MST will be beside Harper Creek for 3.3 miles. ◖

11.2 Trail enters open mature forest with possible campsites. ▲ ◖

11.3 Cross the creek from east (north) to west (south), rock-hopping.

▲ Camping   🛏 Lodging   ℗ Parking   🍽 Food   🚻 Restrooms   🏪 Supplies   ◖ Water   ⛱ Picnic

11.7 Picturesque picnic spot. For the next 0.1 mile, the trail stays on a steep slope beside the creek as it crashes through the cascades and among large rock outcrops below. The trail is 50 feet above the creek; here it flows as a white sheet of water over the rocks.

12.1 Enter an extensive camping area under hollies before crossing the creek from west to east.

12.2 Cross back from east to west and reach a level open area on the west side with a campsite big enough for 1 or 2 tents.

12.4 Cross creek again, from west to east.

12.5 Reach a wide spot under mature hardwoods with fire rings and camping spots.

12.6 Cross the creek from east (north) to west (south), rock-hopping and then cross back to the east side in a shallow spot, going right, downstream.

13.1 Enter an open mature hardwood forest with level camping spots 30-50 feet from the creek.

13.4 Cross the creek from east to west.

13.7 You may see signs of a railroad including rails and a railbed. Reach a camping spot and fire ring and then cross the creek to the east side.

13.8 Trail crosses small stream flowing left to right and passes by a level camping spot as it follows a sunny overgrown margin of the creek.

13.9 Pass good campsites before the gorge narrows and the trail descends, separating some from the creek.

14.2 Trail is 30 yards or more above the creek on an old railroad bed. Below is Harper Creek Falls, a series of 15-foot falls that may be reached in 100 yards by a trail to the right.

14.4 Descend into an extensive floodplain and heavily used campsite area. Go right around the western edge of the clearing to cross Harper Creek. Staying left, on the north side of this camping area is the Harper Creek Trail (FST 260), which leads 1.3 miles to parking on Brown Mtn. Beach Rd. (SR 1328), which parallels Wilson Creek. Harper Creek here is not deep, but it is difficult to rock-hop without getting wet. Continue across to the west side. This is just above the confluence with Raider Camp Creek. You will go upstream on the north side of Raider Camp Creek.

Camping **Lodging** ℗ **Parking** **Food** **Restrooms** **Supplies** **Water** **Picnic**

Harper Creek Trail
Photo by Eileen Kelly

14.9 Enter an open rhododendron valley with lush moss and dog hobble before passing through a floodplain where campsites are plentiful. ▲ 💧

15.4 Continue following the creek upstream, climbing rapidly in places. Reach a floodplain where there is a fire pit and campsite; the trail leaves the creek. ▲ 💧

16.3 Ascend through an open forest of mature hardwoods, predominately poplar, to a saddle where MST crosses a trail following the ridge. Leave the Raider Camp Creek basin to enter the Harper Creek basin. The MST runs conjunctively with blue-blazed Raider Camp Creek Trail (FST 277).

16.6 Round a ridge on the north and east side in a burned-over area of scrubby growth, affording panoramic views of mountains to the north from west to east, including Grandmother and Grandfather Mtns., before entering a mature forest.

16.7 MST goes left and FST 277 (Raider Camp Creek Trail, a blue-blazed connector trail) continues straight, leading 0.2 mile to a cliff overlooking South Harper Creek with a dramatic view into a box canyon and the 250-foot South Harper Falls. On the north side of the creek, approximately 200 feet below is FST 260, which is reachable from FS 58 going to Kawana (a former community designated on Forest Service maps).

16.8 Come to some magnificent large oaks. Good camping spots.

16.9 Past the intersection with the connector trail, MST turns left, leaving an old railroad bed and ascending in a deep narrow gully.

17.0 MST is joined by a trail from the left and follows a broad rounded ridge, ascending gently uphill through mature forest.

17.1 MST passes through rhododendron and mountain laurel as it wraps right across a slope on a narrow ledge, giving views to the northeast before entering open forest, where a trail joins from the right.

18.1 A blue rectangle-blazed trail crosses MST and goes left to Chestnut Mtn. MST emerges onto an old road, which will widen and continue for 0.5 mile.

18.8 Trail reaches an improved parking area and passes through a gate. Blazes may be hard to find here due to overgrowth, but the trail follows a north-south corridor along the old roadbed.

18.9 FS 198 forks to the left. Go right and pass through a gate. This area, with good campsites, is known as Wilderness Camp. Although you will see improved parking here, vehicle travel on FS 198 is generally blocked at FS 982 to prevent travel on an extremely rough road.

20.7 Trail is following the south and east slope with occasional views across the valley to Chestnut Mtn. The slope is steep to the left while the trail moves in and out of deciduous forest and rhododendron thickets.

Camping Lodging Parking Food Restrooms Supplies Water Picnic

20.8 Trail crosses one of many small creeks, some with culverts, some with timbers.

21.1 Trail levels out into open forest of poplars and maples.

21.3 After passing through a rhododendron tunnel, the trail reaches Upper Creek. It goes upstream a short way before crossing, where rock-hopping is possible. The trail then goes left downstream. 💧

21.4 Come to an area with many good campsites, which is known as Greentown from the post office that existed here during logging days. There are many side trails. The trail goes away from Upper Creek along a small tributary. It ascends with this creek for the next 0.5 mile. 🔺 💧

21.6 Trail follows the south side of a slope and crosses a small spring.

21.9 Trail ascends with the creek along rock outcrops that make nice picnic spots.

22.0 After passing through level open forest with good camping spots, the trail crosses a small creek flowing right to left into the main creek and begins to climb.

22.3 Climb beside a small creek on the left before turning left and crossing a saddle. The trail will follow the north side of the ridge. 💧

22.4 Ascend in a 2-3-foot-deep washed-out gully and emerge into a wildlife field.

22.5 Past the wildlife field, MST passes through rhododendron before reaching NC 181 where there is parking on the east side. This is just north of MP 21. The trail continues over the guardrails to the other side, where it follows FS 496, which is usually open to vehicle travel. The trail will be on the gravel road the next 1.2 miles. It is 5.0 miles north on NC 181 to general store and post office; 10.0 miles to full-service private campgrounds. 🔺 Ⓟ 🛒

23.3 Pass a fire ring and campsite on the left where the old MST comes in. You can take this side trip to Steels Creek Falls. 🔺

23.7 Leave FS 496, going left to pass through a locked gate. Parking is possible. Ⓟ

23.8 An old trail goes left. Stay right, pass through a notch, and reach the end of the road spur from FS 496.

23.9 Trail makes a moderate descent out on a ridge.

24.2 Descend the ridge dividing Steels Creek and Gingercake Creek to a pine, magnolia, and oak forest where the trail reaches good camping sites and Steels Creek.

24.6 Re-cross Steels Creek.

24.8 MST, on an old road, goes right when the road forks.

24.9 Cross Steels Creek and reach tributary Gingercake Creek, where there is good camping.

25.0 On the old road, MST passes a wildlife field with apple trees on the right.

25.5 Trail goes through open forest of maples and poplars with lush fern ground cover.

25.8 Descend on switchbacks, to a floodplain on Steels Creek with good camping spots. Steels Creek Falls is 100 yards upstream from the camping area and worth the side trip. It will require climbing over boulders.

26.1 Trail stays up and away from the creek on the west side, descending with it as it falls, sometimes rapidly. The trail and creek are forced together in a narrows. Signage here may not be visible; follow along the creek—do not cross it.

26.3 Trail leaves Steels Creek just before Buck Creek joins it from the right. Go upstream beside Buck Creek a short distance. Many fishing trails lead downstream.

26.4 Cross Buck Creek. The trail remains in a floodplain where there is good camping.

26.5 Begin an ascent from the floodplain.

26.7 Another trail on an old road crosses MST. Follow the blazes. MST stays on the south side of the ridge.

26.8 Trail cuts back right (south) to follow the ridge, leaving the sound of the creek. It will stay on top of the ridge for 0.1 mile.

26.9 Trail is on the north side of the ridge.

27.3 Small streams and springs cross the trail during wet season.

27.6 Trail is squeezed beside rock faces on the left and a steep rhododendron slope to the right.

27.7 Trail enters an opening in the forest with a fire pit on the right, a possible camping spot.

Camping Lodging Parking Food Restrooms Supplies Water Picnic

27.9 MST goes right. Straight is FS 210C, which may be overgrown and impassable.

28.2 Leave a cove and ascend sharply into rhododendron before reaching a level section.

28.3 Round a ridge and begin climbing again.

28.5 Reach a knob where you can hear Buck Creek to the right.

28.9 MST arrives at FS 496 close to its intersection with FS 210 on the left. Go right onto FS 496. Ⓟ

29.0 Leave FS 496 and go left ascending along a tributary of Buck Creek. 💧

29.4 Reach FS 210. Go right on it about 200 feet before turning left.

29.6 MST leaves the creek and passes through a campsite where an old road goes right to Spence Ridge Trail (FST 233) and FS 210. Begin a moderate ascent to Table Rock on a series of wooden steps in open mature forest. ⛺ 💧

29.8 The ascent slows somewhat. Looking back you may get a view of Hawksbill.

30.5 MST joins Table Rock Trail, which goes left to the summit of Table Rock. Go right and in less than 100 yards, MST and Table Rock Trail turn left. Straight is Little Table Rock Trail (FST 236), which follows the ridge down. Right, a trail goes down the mountainside to a spring, which may be last water source before Linville River. 💧

30.9 Reach the south side of the Table Rock parking lot where there are trash receptacles, vault toilets, and picnic tables, but no water. On FS 210, it is 13 miles to NC 181. MST continues on the south side of the parking lot. Ⓟ 🚻

31.1 Ascend into an extensive and heavily used camping area. ⛺

31.2 On top of the ridge, begin passing among the Chimneys, remarkable shapes and stacks of rock. Dramatic views in all directions.

31.3 Trail is on the west side of the ridge with views into gorge.

31.6 Trail turns left (east) and begins to descend.

32.1 Dramatic overlook with a view of the east side of the ridge up to Table Rock.

32.4 Leave a small saddle and descend rapidly.

32.5 Reach an extensive campsite in the gap without a reliable water source. ⛺

⛺ Camping 🛏 Lodging Ⓟ Parking 🍴 Food 🚻 Restrooms 🛒 Supplies 💧 Water 🏕 Picnic

Lake James
Photo by Christine White

32.6 Leave the camping area.

32.7 Pass through an area of severely burned pine, where all big trees are dead.

32.9 Reach a saddle where there are campsites.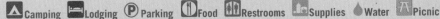

33.1 Steady moderate climb.

33.2 Reach the ridge top and junction with Cambric Trail (FST 234), which is not always maintained. That trail goes right on the ridge (west) into the gorge. Go left.

33.3 Pass a fire ring on the ridge.

33.5 Reach the top of small knob.

33.6 Trail follows a ridge with dramatic views to the north.

34.2 Trail's ascent ends. It will not climb again until past the Linville River in about 4.5 miles.

34.4 Here there are views north of the Chimneys and Table Rock. Make a slight descent from the ridge and stay level for the next 2.2 miles.

35.7 Trail passes through a desolate burned-over area with lots of downed wood and charred trunks, where mountain laurel is the only live vegetation of any size.

35.9 Pass an unusual pond, which is often dry, on top of the mountain.

36.0 As the ridge narrows, trail follows the rim where one can see down into the gorge with views of the Linville River and mountain ranges to the west.

36.1 MST goes through some rhododendron and some large living oaks. Area is level with camping spots. Lake James is in view. Reach a junction where MST goes right to the west side of the ridge; there are extraordinary views from Shortoff Mtn. An alternate trail goes straight. It rejoins MST beyond Shortoff Mtn. in 0.8 mile.

36.2 Leave the campsites and traverse the rounded summit, heading west and then south to the lip of the gorge where there are breathtaking views into the gorge and across the river to the Black Mtns. in the west.

36.5 Trail follows a narrow passage, across a crevice and past a seep that is a possible but not abundant water source.

36.6 Leave the gorge and begin a descent of 1,700 feet in the next 1.7 miles to the Linville River. The trail turns back east.

36.7 Trail goes east away from the gorge.

36.9 MST turns right. Left is the alternate trail that traverses the east side of Shortoff Mtn. Straight is a trail that leads to a parking area on Wolf Pit Rd. coming off NC 126 in about 1.0 mile. Go right on MST and descend toward the Linville River. Ⓟ

37.0 Trail descends on the left (east) side of the ridge spine.

37.8 Looking back right, you can see the face of Shortoff Mtn.

38.1 A blue-dot trail (Linville River Connector Trail) joins from the left (east). *Note:* This connector trail forms an alternate route to avoid fording the Linville River if it is too high to cross safely. On the connector trail, it is 2.5 miles to NC 126, a possible access point. The NC 126 access location is at a locked gate at the entrance to NC Wildlife Game Lands. There is limited parking here. After the 2.5-mile walk to NC 126, it is 0.7 mile to the right on NC 126 to Parks Drive, which is across the Linville River Bridge, then right on Parks

Drive for 0.3 mile to where the road is gated and crosses private land for 0.9 mile before joining MST at WB Mile 38.6. (P)

38.3 Reach the east side of the Linville River after a steady descent. MST goes left downstream. 🌢

38.4 Pass through heavily used campsites and beside fire rings to reach a river crossing. The river is about 60 yards wide here and typically no more than knee high. 🔺 🌢

38.4 Reach the west bank of the Linville River. Go left downstream.

38.5 Reach the "Boy Scout" campsite beside the river. MST goes right, away from the river. 🔺 🌢

38.6 Reach a private road running along the river. Left, in 0.9 mile is Parks Drive and 0.3 mile further, NC 126. There is no public access here. MST goes right (north) on the road and then left in a few hundred yards, out of the river floodplain to begin ascending the western side of Linville Gorge.

39.3 After a gentle-to-moderate climb, reach the top of a knob in thick young pines with dramatic views of Shortoff Mtn. across the river.

39.5 Descend the knob to a tributary of the Linville River.

39.7 Cross the creek, going left.

39.8 Continue upstream. Another creek will join from the left, and then a trail comes in from the left.

40.0 Leave the creek and begin a strenuous climb to a saddle in open forest. 🌢

40.1 Reach a saddle and go left on MST up the ridge. Another trail goes right on the ridge.

40.3 Make a strenuous climb to views of Lake James and Shortoff Mtn. back to the east.

40.5 After a gentle ascent on the ridge, begin a moderate-to-strenuous climb up a burned-over slope with little shade.

40.9 Reach the Pinnacle. MST skirts it to the north, but just past it, a trail goes left a short way to an observation platform and rock outcrop with spectacular views to the east, south, and west. Continue west on a heavily used trail to Old NC 105 (SR 1328, also called Kistler Memorial Hwy.).

41.2 Reach Old NC 105 and a small parking area. MST goes left, down the road, for 0.8 mile. (P)

Camping Lodging Parking Food Restrooms Supplies Water Picnic

Linville Gorge ledge
Photo by Chris Adkins

42.0 MST goes right, off the road, at a small parking area. Ⓟ

42.0 MST joins an old road and makes a gradual descent.

42.3 Reach 2 small creeks. MST on the old road stays east of them and will continue to descend with the creek. 🌢

43.0 Cross a stream just below the juncture of two small streams and ascend on a deeply rutted old road. 🌢

43.2 Reach a nice campsite and go right on a larger old road that is the Overmountain Victory Trail. ▲

43.4 Reach FS 106 (Dobson Knob Rd.), where the MST goes left. The Overmountain Victory Trail goes straight across FS 106 and through a gate. Go left on FS 106.

43.7 Follow FS 106 and pass a gated wildlife field on the right with vehicle parking.

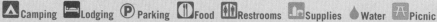

Camping Lodging Ⓟ Parking Food Restrooms Supplies 🌢 Water Picnic

44.7 Reach a communication tower, then two more.

44.8 Reach a parking area providing access. Pass through a gate at the end of FS 106. Ⓟ

45.3 Campsite on right at a bend in the road. ▲

45.4 Continue on the road, which is badly rutted.

46.0 Pass a wildlife field on the right.

46.5 Reach an intersection of rutted roads. There are campsites here. MST stays right, passes another wildlife field on the right, and enters rhododendrons. ▲

46.7 Still on an old road, begin an easy-to-moderate climb.

46.8 A trail goes right. MST stays left.

46.9 Trail is fairly level here; the road peters out.

47.0 Make a gradual ascent on a streambed, then on moss. This is the last water until you are past Bald Knob. ⬤

47.5 Trail reaches the top of Dobson Knob, where there is a fire ring and a one-tent campsite. Trail continues on top of the ridge. ▲

47.6 Leave the ridge to the left (east).

47.7 Make a rapidly descending sag east in open forest before climbing back to the next knob.

47.8 Regain the ridge after a moderate-to-strenuous climb.

48.0 On the ridge, make a moderate climb through rhododendrons up the north end of Bald Knob.

48.1 Reach a series of dramatic rock outcrops with views to the west. On top of the spine, the trail has only gradual changes in elevation.

48.3 Begin a descent on the ridge down the south side of Bald Knob. There are views of Lake James and the east.

48.4 Trail goes right, leaving a rugged fire road that runs up the spine.

48.7 Start a series of rapid switchbacks down to reach the top of a ridge.

48.9 Make a moderate descent on top of the ridge, and come to the end where an overlook to the left gives dramatic views to the south. Trail goes right, off the ridge onto another series of rapid switchbacks.

49.0 Reach a rock outcrop with a spectacular view to the north and west. Looking uphill (east and north) you see Bald Knob; above and beyond (northeast) is Dobson Knob.

49.3 Make a moderate descent, where the trail is narrow on a steep slope.

49.5 Pass a strange sinkhole on the right (uphill) side of the trail.

▲ Camping 🛏 Lodging Ⓟ Parking 🍴 Food 🚻 Restrooms 🏪 Supplies ⬤ Water 🪑 Picnic

49.6 Reach a spot with a view to the west across the valley up to the Blue Ridge. The descent is easy to moderate.

49.8 Cross a rocky intermittent streambed and join a ridge top.

50.0 Ridge is narrow and rock-strewn in places with easy-to-moderate descent.

50.3 Trail leaves the back of the ridge, going right into open forest. In this area there are several good camping spots. ⛺

50.5 Short path on left to a piped spring. 💧

50.6 On an old road following a creek, emerge from a hollow and arrive at a more recent, but still old, road and go left.

51.0 The road makes a gradual descent, following the contours of the base of Bald Knob. As it makes turns around the mountain, there are occasional views of the valley of the North Fork of the Catawba River, which the trail will cross.

51.4 MST leaves the old road, going right and begins a moderate descent.

51.6 Cross a railroad and approach the river.

51.7 Reach a nice 200-foot pedestrian bridge crossing the North Fork of the Catawba River and arrive at an old road along the river. The crossing point for waders before the bridge was built is 0.1 mile downstream. Go left on the road. 💧

52.0 Continue downstream in the floodplain.

52.3 Going right, away from the river, the trail crosses a gravel maintenance road and passes under power lines. It continues across a field to a gate at its edge. Pass through the gate on the road.

52.6 Reach a creek and leave the floodplain. Continue on the road, ascending gradually for 0.3 mile.

52.9 MST leaves the road to the right and begins a moderate climb.

53.7 Reach the top of the knob, which is circled by an old road. Stay right and emerge onto a grassy area where there is good camping. ⛺

53.8 Several roads intersect in the grassy area. Continue across and reach FS 150.

54.0 Follow FS 150 down the hill, then take a right onto FS 149.

54.3 Take a left, leaving FS 149.

54.6 Descend through a pine forest, ending with a switchback.

55.0 Reach a wildlife field. After skirting it to the right (north and east), make a short descent into rhododendrons and cross a normally dry streambed.

55.2 Emerge from rhododendrons onto a possible parking area at the end of a rough (four-wheel drive advised) but traveled road that leads to US 221. *Note:* The gate for this road may be locked. Check with the ranger station at 828-652-2144 if you are hoping to park there. Ⓟ

55.5 Reach US 221. To the left (south) it is 2.0 miles to a general store; 4.0 miles to all amenities. To the right (north) it is 0.8 mile to a convenience store. Cross US 221 onto Green Mtn. Rd. next to the USFS Work Center at Woodlawn. To the left is a parking lot and restrooms. Ⓟ 🚻 🛒 🛏 🍴

55.6 MST takes a few switchbacks from the parking lot to a field and then passes through stanchions on a road, leaving the park. Continue on this road for 1.0 mile.

56.6 Leave the road, going right.

56.8 Round the end of the ridge.

57.5 Leave the old road and go right.

57.7 Make a gradual descent on the west side of Grassy Knob before reaching a floodplain and joining a wide trail. Go upstream along Tom's Creek. Cross it, then cross a smaller tributary and arrive at a well-traveled road. Go left on the road for 0.8 mile in the Tom's Creek floodplain. 💧

58.5 100 yards after crossing a designated wild-trout stream, flowing right to left on a concrete ford, leave the road to the right and begin an ascent on switchbacks.

58.9 Make a moderate climb on the ridge. A road will join the trail from the left.

59.0 Trail has been on an old road on a wide corridor, which narrows as it returns to the ridgeback.

59.2 Leave rhododendron from the north side of the ridge, cross the ridge, and ascend through open forest past interesting rock outcrops.

59.7 Continue a gradual ascent through open hardwood forest to a sharp right turn in the trail onto the ridge going north. An old road departs to the left. MST continues straight on the ridge.

🔺 Camping   🛏 Lodging   Ⓟ Parking   🍴 Food   🚻 Restrooms   🛒 Supplies   💧 Water   🅰 Picnic

View from atop the Pinnacle
Photo by Otto Ofanador

59.9 Continue the gradual ascent, passing through nice hardwoods on an old road.

60.3 Pass through scrubby burned-over pines.

60.8 Lake Tahoma is visible to the south as MST ascends gradually on the contour.

61.0 Trail ascends moderately, then gradually, on an old road to a ridge and a gap where there is a fire ring.

61.2 Trail ascends moderately north and west before wrapping around the south end of the ridge.

61.3 Climb gradually on the right (east) side of the ridge. In winter, there are good views to the east and southeast.

61.6 Trail is wide, making a gradual ascent on the rounded ridge, before narrowing and becoming steeper.

61.8 A trail to the right leads to the site of the Woods Mtn. Lookout Tower. The only vestiges of the tower are the four concrete corner footings.

Camping Lodging ⓟ Parking Food Restrooms Supplies ◆ Water Picnic

61.9 Trail goes north on the east side of the knob and then takes a sharp left to round the north side before making a rapid descent on the ridgeback.

62.1 Crossing on a narrow ridge, ascend around the peak of Woods Mtn., before staying level, then descending. In 0.2 mile around the top, there is a fire ring and good views to the north.

62.7 The descent on switchbacks is rapid, then trail becomes more gradual along a ridge.

63.6 Trail climbs to the top of a narrow ridge with views of Lake Tahoma.

64.2 Round a knob on the right, descend to a gap where there is a fire ring, then ascend on top of the ridge.

64.7 Trail descends, switching back on the east side, then levels out going south in rhododendrons.

65.0 Make a moderate descent from one knob to the next, then take switchbacks to climb the next knob.

65.2 Descend moderately from the knob on the north side before reaching a narrow ridge, staying level.

65.3 Skirt around the south side of a knob, then descend to a saddle where a trail crosses.

65.4 Continue on a narrow ridge, reach the south side of a knob, then make a moderate climb.

65.7 On a rounded ridge, reach a saddle, then make an ascent to a rounded knob.

66.2 Make a moderate ascent before rounding the next knob.

66.4 Make a brief ascent and reach the top of a knob with views west to Buck Creek Gap.

66.5 Reach Horse Gap where Armstrong Creek Trail (FST 223) goes north.

66.6 MST follows contours around the south and east side of the knob and makes an easy-to-moderate climb to a saddle.

66.8 Trail joins an old road that comes in from the right and reaches a gap with views south. Continue west through a white gate.

67.1 Leave the ridge and begin a descent to BRP on an old road parallel to BRP.

Camping   Lodging   Parking   Food   Restrooms   Supplies   Water   Picnic

Table Rock becomes a shadow monster
Photo by Brandon Thrower

67.4 Reach BRP at Buck Creek Gap, where the trail goes left onto the parkway and crosses a viaduct that goes over NC 80. It exits past the overpass to the right. There is parking on NC 80 south of BRP. Ⓟ

67.6 Trail follows a ridge, which turns south; BRP passes underneath through a tunnel. Make a gradual descent along the ridge, now on the south (east) side of the parkway.

68.6 Cross BRP again to the north (west) and follow a ridge along it.

69.0 Cross BRP to the south and east and emerge into Singecat Overlook parking area (MP 345.3), where there is daytime access. Leave the parking area on the south and west side and ascend the ridge going west. Ⓟ

69.1 Continue on the ridge south of BRP, heading west.

69.5 Cross the BRP. No parking access.

69.9 Ascend from BRP to a gap, then make a gradual descent.

70.2 Parallel BRP, which appears as a distinctive flat ridge to the south.

70.8 Cross the remnants of an old logging road.

70.9 On a steep slope, the trail goes between boulders and over slick rocks.

71.2 Cross a Roaring Fork tributary, where there is camping downstream to the right. A 4,160-foot rocky peak looms to the south. ▲ ⬧

71.9 Trail goes through the gap between Big Laurel and Big Ridge, leading into the Roaring Fork basin.

72.1 To the northwest, across the valley, a view of the ridge with Balsam, Cattail Peak, Potato Hill, and Winterstar (L-R), all over 5,000 feet.

72.2 Cross over the ridge and enter Neal's Creek basin. You will gradually descend with this ridge, making several wide switchbacks back and forth across its spine. On the ridge, you may hear the sound of the South Toe and have a view of the Neal's Creek bowl.

72.7 Trail widens as it follows an old road, crossing a more gradual slope.

72.9 MST joins the spine of the ridge, coming down from the left. To the north-northwest, across the South Toe River valley, there is a view of Maple Camp Bald and beyond it, 6,000-foot Cattail Peak.

73.0 MST joins an old road coming in from the right.

73.1 Trail continues its descent and offers a view of the Neal's Creek bowl.

73.2 Reach a gate, cross FS 2074 and pass through another gate onto an old logging road.

73.4 Cross bridge over Neal's Creek. Still on the logging road, pass through a gate. ⬧

73.6 MST leaves the old logging road.

73.7 Pass a wildlife field and old apple trees on the right, then cross a rocky wet-weather streambed.

73.8 Cross Lost Cove Creek. ⬧

73.9 MST merges with a logging road, coming from the right, which continues to FS 472.

74.0 Wildlife field on the right.

74.2 The old logging road merges with another old road coming from the right.

74.7 MST leaves the old logging road.

74.9 Green Knob Trail (FST 182) and River Loop Trail (FST 200) join from the left, and the combined trails continue west.

▲ Camping 🛏 Lodging ⓟ Parking 🍴 Food 🚻 Restrooms 🏪 Supplies ⬧ Water ⛱ Picnic

75.2 Arrive at a parking area on FS 472 (South Toe River Rd.) and the western end of Segment 4. *Note*: To reach the parking area by car from the BRP, take NC 80 (at MP 344) toward Burnsville. After the small community of Busick, turn left onto South Toe River Rd. This road will eventually turn to gravel and follow the river. At the gravel road intersection, make a slight turn on the first right. The parking area is on your left just before a bridge and the entrance to the Black Mtn. Campground on the right. See the "Camping on the Trail" section for this segment for information about camping at the Black Mtn. Campground.

FRIENDS OF THE NORTH CAROLINA
MOUNTAINS-to-SEA TRAIL

YES, I'd like to become a Friend of the Mountains-to-Sea Trail!

❑ $20 (Student)

❑ $35 (Basic Membership)

❑ $50

❑ $100

❑ $250

❑ $500*

❑ $1000* (1000-Mile Society)

❑ Please let me know about volunteer opportunities.

❑ My employer will match my gift. I've enclosed a matching gift form.

❑ I know of a group that would like to hear more about the Mountains-to-Sea Trail. Please contact me about speaking opportunities.

❑ I'm interested in making a planned gift. Please send me information about the Allen de Hart Legacy Society.

Name: _____

Mailing Address: _____

City: _____ State: _____ Zip Code: _____

Email address: _____

Phone: _____

How did you first learn about Friends? _____

* Friends who donate at least $1000 or $500 plus 75 hours of volunteer time per year become members of the 1000-Mile Society. Society members receive recognition in Friend's annual report and are invited to a special Society event every year.

Please make check payable to Friends of the MST and mail it with this completed form to:

Friends of the Mountains-to-Sea Trail
P.O. Box 10431
Raleigh, NC 27605

Friends of the MST is a 501(c)3 organization, and donations are tax-deductible. Financial information about Friends of the MST and a copy of its license are available from the NC Charitable Solicitation Licensing Section at 1-888-830-4989. The license is not an endorsement by the state.